DEATH VALLEY

A SCENIC WONDERLAND

BY STEVEN L. WALKER & DOROTHY K. HILBURN

Above: Salt Flats near Badwater, the lowest point in the United States. Death Valley National Park.
PHOTO BY CARR CLIFTON

Below: Salt marsh and the Panamint Range. Death Valley National Park.
PHOTO BY CARR CLIFTON

 CAMELBACK
DESIGN GROUP, INC.

 CANYONLANDS
PUBLICATIONS & INDIAN ART

Designed by Camelback Design Group, Inc., 8655 East Via de Ventura, Suite G200, Scottsdale, Arizona 85258. Phone: 602-948-4233. Distributed by Canyonlands Publications, 4860 North Ken Morey Drive, Bellemont, Arizona 86015. For ordering information please call (520) 779-3888.

Requests for additional information should be made to: Camelback/Canyonlands Venture at the address above, or call our toll free telephone number: 1-800-283-1983.

Library of Congress Catalog Number: 95-70820
International Standard Book Number: 1-879924-23-4

Proudly printed and bound in the U.S.A.

Front Cover: Manly Beacon and the badlands in Golden Canyon bathed in the dawn's twilight. Death Valley National Park.
PHOTO BY JEFF GNASS

Background: Dune crest at Eureka Dunes, a part of the 1994 addition to the new national park.
PHOTO BY CARR CLIFTON

Left: Mesquite and dunes glow in the afternoon sunlight. Death Valley National Park.
PHOTO BY CARR CLIFTON

GOODBYE, DEATH VALLEY...

In December of 1849, a bone-weary group of settlers bound for the California goldfields made the disastrous mistake of attempting to take a short cut through desolate territory they would come to name Death Valley.

A wagon train of approximately 100 wagons strong, known as the "Jayhawker" party, was organized outside of the Mormon community of Salt Lake City. The settlers hired Jefferson Hunt to guide them south towards Los Angeles where they would then head north to the gold-fields of Northern California.

Hunt, an experienced guide who had made several successful trips between Salt Lake City and Southern California, was qualified to lead the party but many of the pioneers decided to leave him believing they had an opportunity to reach their destination weeks sooner than they had originally planned.

Trouble began when Captain Wesley Smith, a member of a passing party, produced a map showing a short cut due west, towards Walker Pass. Hunt urged the party to stay on the original route but several members of the party were quite anxious to get to the goldfields and the riches they were sure awaited them.

Hunt continued south, following the original trail, with only a few wagons following his lead. At first, the majority of the party followed Captain Smith, but many wagons turned back to follow Hunt until he again lead well over half of the wagon train.

Captain Smith's pack train was fast moving and he continued on his way west. Ironically,

Smith later turned back to follow Hunt when he realized the extreme difficulty of the terrain. The slower moving wagons followed but were held up for some time on steep bluffs they named Mt. Misery. Once the settlers were able to continue the journey, several parties split up and took different routes.

One group of Jayhawkers spent a week in Death Valley before finding an escape route. Another group, the Wades, perilously low on supplies, found their way out following the banks of the dry Amargosa River to the south. Richard Culverwell struck out on his own and perished during his attempt to find a way out of Death Valley.

The remaining Jayhawkers entered what is now known as Death Valley on Christmas Day of 1849. A group of single men, unencumbered by women and children, left the group and headed north while several families, including the Bennett and Arcan families, continued west into the valley where they were forced to spend a terrifying five weeks before being rescued. Fates of other parties splintering off remain a mystery and are the subject of numerous historical controversies still today.

John Rogers and William Lewis Manly were young men hired in Salt Lake City as drivers for the Jayhawker party. After the Bennett and Arcan party had failed in an attempt to escape over the mountains to the west, they made camp at a spring near what is today Furnace Creek. Manly scouted the north and west for a route from the valley only to return with the

Death Valley earned its name in the winter of 1850, as the last remaining members of the Bennett-Arcan party were leaving the valley after five weeks of incredible hardship. One woman, turning to look back at the valley one last time, was heard to say "Goodbye, Death Valley." The name has endured ever since.

Preceding Pages: Clouds reflecting in a salt sink with the Panamint Range in the background.
PHOTO BY CARR CLIFTON

Left: Clouds above Manly Beacon from Golden Canyon. Manly Beacon was named after William Manly who, along with John Rogers, heroically saved the lives of many California bound settlers trapped in Death Valley in the winter of 1849.
PHOTO BY JEFF FOOTT

Right: Blond grasses, Death Valley National Park.
PHOTO BY CARR CLIFTON

GOODBYE, DEATH VALLEY...

sad tidings that the only hope for escape from Death Valley remaining was to the south.

The remaining pioneers were now down to only four wagons and precious few provisions. They had been forced to abandon wagon after wagon, and the possessions they carried with hopes of a new life in a new land, when they were forced to slaughter their oxen for food in a process that had begun before they even entered Death Valley. Remains of the wagons and their possessions have been found in the desert sands throughout the years in a silent testimony to the plight of the Jayhawkers and their struggle to survive Death Valley.

The nearly exhausted group made camp a day's walk southwest of Furnace Creek at a water hole later named Bennett's Well. After much discussion, it was decided the group's only hope for rescue was to remain in Death Valley while Manly and Rogers, the fittest members of the party, went on for help. The two men headed west, over the Panamint Mountains, on foot searching for Los Angeles which they hoped was but a few days' walk away. They had no way of knowing it was more than 200 miles to the southwest.

The walk to Los Angeles took Manly and Rogers almost two weeks of toil and hardship. After they escaped the valley, they came upon the remains of one of the bachelors who had struck out on his own. He had escaped the confines of the valley but died from the effort, for the journey remaining was little easier than the one he had completed.

When Manly and Rogers arrived in the San Fernando Valley north of Los Angeles, they

were directed to the San Francisco Rancho where they were able to obtain food and fresh horses for their return journey. There was no time for Manly and Rogers to rest or recover, lives of the pioneers in Death Valley depended on their speedy return.

While the settlers awaited Manly and Rogers return, from a journey the consensus thought should be a ten day trip, several lost their faith and struck out on their own, further weakened by the additional time spent in Death Valley. Richard Culverwell was one who had decided

to walk out alone and had perished during his attempt to find a way out. His body was found by Manly and Rogers when they re-entered the valley. The grisly discovery led the two men to wonder if they had indeed been gone too long to save the remaining settlers.

When they came upon the remaining wagons at Bennett's Well there was no sign of life. They had been gone for 25 days, which may have been too long. William Manly fired a shot into the air. Miraculously, people began to appear, overjoyed at the sight of their rescuers.

Although there were only three deaths that were documented in the settlers' ordeal, the valley had tested the limits of endurance of all who had dared to enter it. As the last of the Jayhawkers left the place they had come so close to dying in, a woman turned for one last look and was heard to say, "Goodbye, Death Valley." The name has endured ever since.

Below: Sand patterns and Arrow Weed, Mesquite Flat Sand Dunes. Arrow Weed, growing to 10 feet tall, was used by Indians to make arrow shafts.
PHOTO BY CARR CLIFTON

GEOGRAPHY OF DEATH VALLEY...

Climate...According to the American Heritage Dictionary a desert is: "1. A dry, barren, often sandy region that because of environmental extremes can naturally support little or no vegetation. 2. *Archaic.* A wild uncultivated and uninhabited region. 3. A dismal or forbidding area." Death Valley, with an average annual rainfall of merely 1.84 inches over the past 83 years, certainly qualifies as a desert by the first definition, and early pioneers would have been quick to agree with the third.

HOT, HOT, HOT...

Death Valley may be the hottest place on earth. If it's not, it's a close second.

1913 134°F recorded at **Furnace Creek**,* Death Valley, highest ever recorded at time.

1922 136°F recorded at **Azizia, Libya**, new world record that is still unbroken.

*Furnace Creek was then Greenland Ranch. Temperatures at Badwater, 20 miles south and almost 100 feet lower in elevation, are normally several degrees warmer and may have been hotter on July 10, 1913 than the 134°F recorded at Furnace Creek and hotter than the 136°F record in Libya in 1922.

Death Valley is a desert as a result of several factors. Its location, 37.5 degrees north latitude, places it in a subtropical high, an area under the influence of high pressure systems, as are most the world's deserts which are generally found between 15 and 35 degrees north and south latitudes. The high pressure keeps the air descending and retaining its warmth.

Summer temperatures, which often surpass 120°F, heat the air and as the warm air rises it often evaporates moisture before it can reach the ground. Rain from above can sometimes be seen as virga, wisps of precipitation streaming from a cloud but evaporating before they reach the earth.

The extreme low elevation at Death Valley, 282 ft. below sea level near Devil's Golf Course, is the lowest point in the Western Hemisphere. Lower elevations have higher temperatures. The rainshadow effect of the mountain ranges

TEMPERATURE AND RAINFALL

The chart below shows the average monthly temperatures and rainfall over an eighty-three year period from 1911, the year the permanent weather station was established at Furnace Creek, through 1994. Temperature is recorded in degrees Fahrenheit and rainfall amounts are in inches. The temperatures below were taken in the shade at the Furnace Creek weather station.

MONTH	AVERAGE	AVERAGE MAXIMUM	AVERAGE MINIMUM	HIGHEST	LOWEST	RAINFALL
January	51.8	64.6	39.1	87	15	0.24
February	59.0	72.3	45.6	97	27	0.33
March	66.6	80.4	52.8	102	30	0.24
April	75.9	89.8	61.9	111	35	0.12
May	85.0	99.3	70.7	120	42	0.07
June	94.7	109.0	80.3	128	49	0.03
July	101.6	115.3	87.8	134	52	0.11
August	99.1	113.2	85.0	127	65	0.12
September	90.4	105.8	74.9	120	41	0.11
October	76.8	92.0	61.6	113	32	0.09
November	61.9	75.7	48.1	97	24	0.19
December	52.3	65.1	39.4	86	19	0.19
Annual	76.3	90.1	62.2	134	15	1.84

For every 1,000 feet of additional vertical elevation temperatures will decrease by 3 to 5 degrees. Rainfall figures will also be higher.

Source: Data compiled from Death Valley National Park's daily records and National Weather Service summaries.

GROUND TEMPERATURE...

Death Valley's ground temperature is usually about 40% higher than the air temperature. The hottest ground temperature on record is 201°F at Furnace Creek on July 15, 1972. The air temperature that day reached 128°F.

between Death Valley and the ocean effectively drain clouds of their moisture before reaching the valley. Low elevations and lack of moisture set the stage for one of the hottest places on earth. Extreme heat and low moisture levels, coupled with more than 300 days of sunshine, produce an evaporation rate as high as 150 inches per year, a far cry from the 1.84 inches averaged over the last 83 years.

Left: Cracked mud and scattered needles below tamarisk boughs at Furnace Creek.
PHOTO: JEFF GNASS

Death Valley, 285 miles from Los Angeles and 581 miles from Salt Lake City, has not always been this easy to reach. Flying into Las Vegas and driving down, or an automobile

President Herbert Hoover with a total land area of 1,750,000 acres. March 6, 1937, President Franklin Delano Roosevelt added the Nevada triangle containing an additional 300,000 acres to the national monument. 40 acres at Devil's Hole were added in 1952 by President Harry S Truman to preserve the desert pupfish.

On October 31, 1994, President William Clinton signed the Desert Protection Act, which added 1.3 million acres to Death Valley and changed its designation from a national monument to Death Valley National Park. The act officially protects 95% of the newly formed Death Valley National Park as a wilderness.

A HOP, SKIP, AND A JUMP...

Distances from the Furnace Creek Visitor Center to popular western United States destinations by automobile.

DESTINATION	MILES	KILOMETERS
Baker, CA	112	180
Bakersfield, CA	236	380
Bishop, CA	165	265
Fresno, CA	340	547
Grand Canyon, AZ	432	695
Hoover Dam	177	285
Lake Tahoe, NV	345	552
Las Vegas, NV	120	192
Los Angeles, CA	285	459
Needles, CA	235	376
Phoenix, AZ	478	769
Reno, NV	353	568
Sacramento, CA	506	814
Salt Lake City, UT	581	935
San Diego, CA	341	549
San Francisco, CA	524	873
Sequoia NP, CA	353	568
Yosemite NP, CA	315	504
Zion NP, UT	297	475

Source: National Park Service, Death Valley National Park

trip from many Western states certainly beats a month or two in a covered wagon or walking behind a mule.

Death Valley National Park, with a total land mass of more than 3.3 million acres after recent additions, is the largest national park in the continental United States, surpassed only by national parks in Alaska in terms of total size among the United States' National Parks.

On February 11, 1933, Death Valley became a national monument upon proclamation of

DISTANCES WITHIN THE PARK...

Mileages from the Furnace Creek Visitor Center to destinations within Death Valley National Park by automobile are as follows:

Source: National Park Service, Death Valley National Park

DESTINATION	MILES	DESTINATION	MILES	DESTINATION	MILES
1. Aguereberry Point	46	15. Golden Canyon	3	29. Sand Dunes	19
2. Artists Drive Entrance	9.5	16. Grapevine Ranger Station	50	30. Saratoga Spring	69
3. Badwater	18	17. Harmony Borax Works	2	31. Scotty's Castle	53
4. Butte Valley	52	18. Jubilee Pass	53	32. Skidoo	44
5. Charcoal Kilns	63	19. Keane Wonder Mine	16	33. Stovepipe Wells	24
6. Chloride Cliff	32	20. Leadfield	48	34. Texas Springs Campgd	1.5
7. Dante's View	25	21. Mahogany Flat Campgd	65	35. Thorndyke Campgd	64
8. Daylight Pass	27	22. Mesquite Spring Campgd	52	36. Titus Canyon Trailhead	35
9. Desolation Canyon	5.5	23. Mosaic Canyon	26	37. Towne Pass	40
10. Devil's Golf Course	13	24. Mustard Canyon	2.5	38. Tule Springs	18
11. Devil's Hole	43	25. Natural Bridge	15	39. 20 Mule Team Canyon	5.5
12. Eagle Borax Works	21	26. Panamint Springs	60	40. Ubehebe Crater	56
13. Emigrant Campground	33	27. Racetrack	83	41. Wildrose Campgd	56
14. Eureka Dunes	98	28. Salt Creek	14	42. Zabriskie Point	4.5

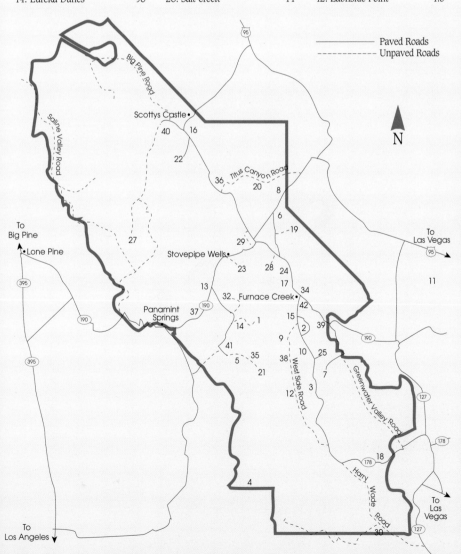

Paved Roads
—————— Unpaved Roads

EARLY INHABITANTS

Four distinct Native American cultures have been identified as occupants of Death Valley in succession for more than 9,000 years. The earliest, the Nevares Spring culture, were spear throwers. They were succeeded by the Mesquite Flat culture, who arrived in the region around 5,000 years ago and used spears and atlatls. They were replaced by the Saratoga Springs culture who introduced the bow and arrow. The final culture, the Shoshone, have occupied the Death Valley region since about A.D. 1100.

The earliest inhabitants of North America migrated from Asia via an ancient land bridge across the Bering Strait during the Pleistocene Epoch, or Ice Age, at least 11,000 years ago and perhaps as many as 37,000 years ago, or more. The exposed land bridge allowed grazing animals and early hunters access to the New World in migrations that lasted until the end of the last Ice Age, around 11,000 years ago.

The first of these Native Americans arrived in the area we now call Death Valley somewhere around 9,000 years ago, or possibly earlier. During this period the valley was far different than it is today. A huge lake, called Lake Manly by geologists today, covered the desert floor and rainfall in the region was plentiful enough to provide adequate forage for giant sloths, mastodons and other animals of the Holocene Era. As the Ice Age glaciers retreated back to the poles, Lake Manly dried up and the region turned into the desert we find today.

Archeologists have identified four distinct prehistoric Native American cultures that have been found in Death Valley. The earliest, the Nevares Spring culture, were hunter-gatherers who built semi-circular stone shelters and fire pits near springs and may have inhabited the valley year-round. Changing climate patterns may have caused them to abandon the area.

The Mesquite Flat culture inhabited the area from a period beginning approximately 5,000 years ago and ending somewhere around the birth of Christ. The Mesquite Flat people were also hunters and gatherers, using spears and atlatls (a rigid board around two feet long with a notch near the top in which the shaft of a spear, dart or arrow, was inserted. The length of the atlatl extended the arm and increased the force behind the throwing of the projectile.) The projectile points found at the later sites are markedly different from those found in Nevares Spring culture sites. The presence of other tools, including some grinding tools, suggest that the Mesquite Flats people may have relied more heavily on gathering nuts, seeds and berries to supplement their diets than their predecessors.

The Saratoga Spring culture entered Death Valley sometime around 2,000 years ago. The lake had long dried up and these newer people were forced to be more resourceful in their hunting and gathering. Projectile points from this period show the use of the bow and arrow which was much more effective in hunting the smaller game thought to be prevalent during this period. The presence of metates, manos and pestles at Saratoga Spring sites show an increase of plant foods in the daily diet.

The Shoshone culture may have overlapped the Saratoga Spring culture and is thought to have begun around A.D. 1100. They were a semi-nomadic people that made pottery, set small game traps, made jewelry and traded with other tribes. The Shoshone were present in the valley during the arrival of the first white settlers and passerbys. The Timbisha Shoshone still inhabit the region today, living year-round in the Furnace Creek area.

Left: Devil's Golf Course reflects Telescope Peak and the Panamint Range. Salt saturated water on the valley floor is reminiscent of Lake Manly, the Pleistocene Era lake that gave sustenance to the earlier Native American cultures that inhabited Death Valley.
PHOTO BY LARRY ULRICH

Right: Petroglyphs in the Cottonwood Mountains. Petroglyphs were made by scratching images into mineral stained rock surfaces. Pictographs were created by painting on rock surfaces and are rarely found in the Death Valley region.
PHOTO BY LARRY ULRICH

GEOLOGY CONTINUED...

forms as we now know them including man's earliest ancestors, horses, camels, canines and other mammals. The earliest rocks in the earth's

Above: White calcite formations form an interesting contrast with the darker limestone rock of Titus Canyon in the Grapevine Mountains. The mountains were covered by as much as 1200 feet of volcanic ash during the late Oligocene and early Miocene epochs.
PHOTO BY JEFF FOOTT

history have long since disappeared through a process known as the rock cycle.

Rock material exposed at the earth's surface by uplift, volcanic activity or water erosion is constantly exposed to further forces of erosion. Water erosion breaks the rock material into smaller and smaller pieces that are transported, by water or wind, to the sea.

These sediments are then deposited on the sea floor where they continue to grow deeper and deeper as additional materials are added until the sedimentary layers become so thick, and reach such tremendous weight, that they may cause the region to sag, forming a geosyncline. When this downwarping is continued over a long period of time, the resulting pressure will cement the sedimentary layers into new formations, which are *sedimentary* rock formations.

At depths of more than 25 miles, deep metamorphism, from very high pressures and extreme temperatures, causes re-crystallization, converting the original sediments into complex new rock types. The new *metamorphic* rock formations may later find their way to the surface through seismic events that start their uplift cycle to the surface.

Partial melting deep within the earth's crust generates new granitic magma, which is in a molten state and migrates upward or laterally. These magmas then extrude through surface fissures or volcanoes, forming formations of *igneous* rock. Once at the surface, the ravages of time and the elements of erosion start the rock cycle all over again.

All three of the basic rock types; sedimentary,

Above: The vista from Dante's View of the white salt pans of Badwater, near the lowest elevations in Death Valley and the United States.
PHOTO BY TOM DANIELSEN

metamorphic and igneous, are present in Death Valley. The older formations were deposited during the Precambrian Era, more than a billion years ago, and can be seen in the form of gneisses, marbles, shists and other metamorphic formations which previously had been sedimentary layers of sandstone, limestones,

GEOLOGY

Death Valley sand dunes, reaching as high as 700 feet, are the largest in California. Sand dunes are created as winds, blowing a minimum of 10 miles per hour to move the finest grains of dry sand, move the grains of sand along in a process called saltation. The larger grains bounce along the ground, seldom rising more than six feet into the air, and dislodge other sand particles which in turn take flight. Wind speed, duration and direction and the size, uniformity and quantity of sand determine the shape of the dune and the patterns on its surface.

Geology is the scientific study of the origin, history and structure of the earth. As its study is broken down into the earth's various regions, new discoveries uncovered in a particular area will often lead to observations that may either reinforce existing points of view or shed an entirely new light on the subject. More than a billion years of Earth's history lies exposed in Death Valley's barren landscape, providing an excellent opportunity to observe the geologic processes responsible for creating the mountains and the valley floor.

Unlike most valleys, carved as rivers wind their way to lower ground, Death Valley is a fault basin, the result of portions of the earth's crust dropping below others as earthquakes caused movements along fault lines, a common occurrence in the valley's past that continues to shape the valley today.

Just two thousand years ago an earthquake thought to have been more powerful than the 1906 San Francisco Earthquake (estimated at 8.3 on the Richter scale), rolled through Death Valley. It left behind a ten foot cliff, called a scarp, that illustrates the drop that occurred in the valley floor. The cliff can be seen along the road from Furnace Creek to Badwater.

Death Valley has experienced fracturing by seismic forces for more than 35 million years, forming as earth's plates rose and fell along fault lines forming the Basin and Range, one of twelve major geologic provinces found in the United States. Basin and Range topography features the parallel mountain ranges of eastern California and Nevada that first defined the region, more than 100 years ago, as a series of mountains and the broad valleys, or basins, that separated them.

The entire region surrounding Death Valley–from parts of southern Oregon and Idaho, almost all of Nevada along with a large part of western Utah, to the eastern California region that includes Death Valley National Park–is part of the Great Basin, an area defined by its true basin properties, not a single river escapes the 250,000 square mile "basin" to reach the sea. The myriad mountain ranges of the Basin and Range relieve storms of precipitation before they reach Death Valley.

Underlying the surface deposits of rock and sand, salts and other mineral deposits are the rock formations of the earth's past. We are able to judge the age of the underlying deposits, where they have become visible, and to date them using a radiometric dating process that determines the age of a rock by measuring the radioactive particles remaining in a sample.

Geologic time is divided into four main eras: the Precambrian, from the beginning of time until 600 million years ago as signified by the appearance of the first hard-shelled fossils; the Paleozoic, from 600 million years ago to 225 million years ago featuring early life forms and the emergence of fish in the fossil record; the Mesozoic, from 225 million years ago to 65 million years ago, the age of the dinosaurs and early mammals; and the Cenozoic, from 65 million years ago until the present with life

Preceding Pages: The valley floor in front of the Panamint Mountains displays intricate salt patterns on its cracked surface.
PHOTO BY JACK DYKINGA

Left: Desert Holly and rocks in Mosaic Canyon on a winter morning. Death Valley National Park.
PHOTO BY JEFF GNASS

Right: The Funeral Mountains are reflected in salt pools on the valley's floor.
PHOTO BY CARR CLIFTON

About Time...

Geology is the scientific study of the origin, history, and structure of the earth. All studies are based on the division and the sub-division of historical geology into eras, periods and epochs...

PRECAMBRIAN	BEGINNING	ENDING
Archeozoic	older than 4 billion years	
Proterozoic	4 billion	600
PALEOZOIC		
Cambrian	600	500
Ordovician	500	425
Silurian	425	400
Devonian	400	345
Mississippian	345	320
Pennsylvanian	320	280
Permian	280	225
MESOZOIC		
Triassic	225	190
Jurassic	190	135
Cretaceous	135	65
CENOZOIC		
TERTIARY		
Paleocene	65	54
Eocene	54	38
Oligocene	38	26
Miocene	26	12
Pliocene	12	1.7
QUATERNARY		
Pleistocene	1.7	10,000 years
Holocene	10,000 years to present	

shales etc., that were then altered by heat and pressure miles beneath the surface and rose with the mountain ranges. The mountains of the Death Valley region are not all comprised of the same materials. The Funeral Mountains contain deposits of dolomite from the Paleozoic Era, the Panamints contain late Precambrian and Paleozoic sedimentary deposits. The Black Mountains have Cenozoic sedimentary and volcanic rocks and fossilized corals from the Devonian period can be found on the peaks of the Cottonwood Mountains.

During the late Precambrian Era a warm, shallow sea covered Death Valley Basin, laying silt, sand and other debris that formed sedimentary deposits that were thousands of feet thick. Igneous rocks intruded between the sedimentary layers of the deposits. Finally, the weight of these layers caused the basin to sink to lower levels.

During the Paleozoic Death Valley was covered by another shallow sea that deposited trilobites, crinoids, brachiopods, corals and gastropods in limestone deposits that may have been up to sixteen thousand feet thick. During this era, there was little seismic activity.

The Mesozoic Era found increased faulting and the intrusion of granite and other igneous rocks into the earlier sedimentary deposits. The Mesozoic was also the period dinosaurs roamed the earth, although none of their fossils have been uncovered in the Death Valley area.

It was during this era that most of the gold, silver and other metal deposits were laid.

During the Cenozoic Era, volcanic activity covered most of the Death Valley area with a

Above: Ubehebe Crater was formed as magma met ground-water beneath the surface resulting in a steam explosion. PHOTO: LARRY ULRICH

rhyolitic ash, which is the chemical equivalent of granite. Death Valley as we know it began

Below: The colorful deposits of Artists Palette at the base of the Black Mountains are the result of mineral oxidization. Reds, browns and oranges are iron; the purple shades are manganese and the greens are thought to be mica. PHOTO: JEFF FOOTT

to be formed after these volcanic deposits were laid somewhere around 30 million years ago.

Faulting began along the Furnace Creek fault zone and the Black Mountains began to rise about 14 million years ago. The Artist Drive Formation was deposited in layers 4,000 ft. thick around this time.

The Furnace Creek Formation, formed between the Black and Funeral mountains during the Pliocene, gives us many of the multi-colored formations in the area. Boron is found in this formation. Borates are water soluble and were formed as lakes dried up and left borate minerals behind.

The Funeral Formation saw continued mountain building in the region and new formations of mud, sand, volcanic rock and conglomerates in which the remains of mastodons, sabertoothed cats, camels and horses have been found.

During the Pleistocene epoch great sheets of

ice advanced on North America, moving rock great distances and changing environments on

four major occasions. The last Ice ago ended around 10,000 years ago.

Ubehebe Crater was formed as molten rock close to the surface met ground water and turned to steam, increasing pressure and causing a tremendous explosion. The smaller craters in the vicinity are evidence of the same activity. Ubehebe Crater is only a few thousand years old, and the smaller craters are even younger.

The geology of Death Valley has been one of constant change. From mountain building stages and movements along the fault zones to volcanic activity and forces of erosion filling the basin for future deposits, Death Valley continues to re-form in a never ending cycle, one that is only now being truly understood by man.

Below: Rock trails in Racetrack Playa. Water flows into this fine silt basin, but has no escape. The resultant mud is slick enough to allow the wind to sail rocks across the surface.
PHOTO BY: JEFF FOOTT

Above: Sunrise on the rock-hard salt deposits of Devil's Golf Course at the center of the valley.
PHOTO BY LARRY ULRICH

Right: Sand dunes and pickleweed at Mesquite Flat at dusk. Dunes are shaped by the speed, duration and direction of the wind and the size, uniformity and amount of the sand.
PHOTO BY JEFF GNASS

FLORA AND FAUNA

With over 970 species of plants and several hundred species of animals, Death Valley could realistically be considered a valley of life. Variation in elevation stretches from mountain peaks reaching 11,000 feet high to a below sea level depth of 282 feet, creating a wide range of habitat for plant and animal life.

In the study of ecology, the science dealing with all living things, there have been established seven life zones between the Equator and the North Pole. The study of life zones was formulated by Clinton Hart Merriam, one of the worlds greatest naturalists, for the Department of Agriculture. Merriam's premise is that a change of 1000 feet in elevation would have the same effect on plant life as a change of 300-500 miles in latitude. He also determined that temperature drops 3½ to 5 degrees for each 1000 foot rise in elevation. C. Hart Merriam was a member of the 1891 Death Valley expedition undertaken by fellow naturalists, George Bird Grinnell, Frederick Vernon Coville, T. S. Palmer and Vernon Bailey, to study the natural history of Death Valley.

According to Merriam's guidelines there are six life zones within Death Valley National Park. The lowest is the Dry Desert zone of below 500 feet, and the highest is the Hudsonian zone, found at the 11,000 foot level of Telescope Peak.

In the Dry-Desert zone lies the area below sea level which seems desolate but has several hundred species of plants. Many plants, known as halophytes (Gr. salt + plant), survive in soil containing high quantities of both salt and alkali. The pickleweed, *Allenrolfia occidentalis*, is one of these plants. Requiring a fairly close water supply the pickleweed can survive in very salty areas. The iodine bush, *Sueda suffrutescens*, wedge-leaf orach, *Atriplex phyllostegia*, and *Tidestromia*, which has silvery white leaves, are other halophytes.

During years of adequate rainfall, the valley floor blooms a in riot of colorful wildflowers. Most of these flowers live for a very short time, leaving behind seeds for the next flowering season. When the desert blooms a flurry of activity takes place by many species of insects including, bees, ants, wasps and butterflies who feed on the nectar of the wildflowers.

Other plants that occupy the lower regions of Death Valley are the desert five spot, *Malvastrum rotundifolium*, which sports five deep red spots on the inside of its cupped petals, the desert star, *Eremiastrum bellioides*, and the turtle back, *Psathyrotes annua*.

As the elevation rises so does the abundance of plant and animal life. The straw top cholla, *Opuntia echinocarpa,* is only one of the many types of cacti growing in the Lower Sonoran life zone. Sharing that zone are the prickly poppy, *Argemone platyceras*, as well as the desert rue, *Thamnosma montana*, which has distinctive purple flowers.

The endangered desert tortoise, *Gopherus agassizi,* with its small head and domed shell, can also be found in the Lower Sonoran life zone in burrows near shady bushes.

Left: Desert sunflower, *Gerea canescens*, and desert sand verbena, *Abronia villosa*, growing among volcanic rock and white sand in Death Valley National Park.
PHOTO BY LARRY ULRICH

Right: Sun strikes a desert sunflower, *Gerea canescens,* thriving on the desert floor.
PHOTO BY CARR CLIFTON

Flora & Fauna Continued...

Plants, including the desert rue, were used for medicinal purposes by Death Valley's early Native Americans who also used the straight points of the arrowweed bush to make shafts for their arrows. The supply of food for the areas early inhabitants was more abundant in the higher elevations than in the arid valley below.

The recent Eureka Valley addition to Death Valley National Monument has created permanent protection for three unique species of plants found nowhere else in the world: Eureka Dunegrass, Eureka Evening Primrose and Eureka Milk-vetch.

Another 100,000 acres of the Northern Panamint Valley was also added to the monument. Included in this addition is Darwin Falls which cascades into a year-round stream to provide a setting

Left: Desert Five Spot, *Malvastrum rotundifolium*, can be found flowering in spring in the desert washes of Death Valley.
PHOTO BY JEFF FOOTT

Above: Pickleweed, *Allenrolfea occidentalis*, shown here at Salt Creek, is one of the most salt-tolerant plants. It can survive up to six percent salinity in its water supply.
PHOTO BY MICHAEL COLLIER

Death Valley Wildlife...

From 282 feet below sea level to the highest mountain peaks, Death Valley National Park preserves and protects hundreds of species of animal life. The most common image of Death Valley, by the uninitiated, is that of a lack of life. Nothing could be further from the truth.

Although only a few of the many species, such as the coyote or the raven, with its gleaming black feathers, are regularly seen by the casual observer there is plenty of wildlife to be found in the valleys and surrounding areas.

The largest mammal in the area is the majestic desert bighorn sheep, a shy animal with spectacular curved horns, usually seen only by adventurous hikers who explore back canyons and higher elevations of the valley. Another large animal found in Death Valley is the burro, a non-indigenous animal originally brought to the valley by miners. The burro population grew to damaging numbers and their overgrazing and fouling of the water supplies threatened desert bighorn habitat. The National Park Service realized the damage the burros were inflicting on the desert and began a live removal program in 1983. Today there are an estimated 200 burros still in the park.

The graceful kit fox can sometimes be seen

Above: Desert Bighorn sheep, *Ovis canadensis*, are well adapted to life in Death Valley. They require little water and do not consume entire plants while grazing.
PHOTO BY JEFF FOOTT

Above: A wild burro.
PHOTO BY JEFF FOOTT

near the floor of the valley as can black tailed jack rabbit, white tailed antelope, ground squirrel, pocket mouse, Ord's kangaroo rat, desert kangaroo rat, Merriam's kangaroo rat, southern grasshopper mouse, deer mouse, brush mouse and the desert woodrat. Many of these animals are nocturnal and all have adapted to the survive the severe conditions within the park.

The area is also a stopping place for many migratory birds. Red-tailed hawks soar over valleys and canyons while robins, wrens and gray warblers often appear in the fall on their migrations.

The valley provides the over 200 types of resident and migratory birds with a plentiful food source of insects and lizards as well as a few snakes.

The many species of lizards include the Mojave fringe-toed lizard, desert iguana, desert spiny lizard, western whiptail, zebra tail lizard and chuckwalla. The chuckwalla is a large lizard that often surpasses 16 inches in length and has a unique way of avoiding capture; it wedges itself between rocks and then puffs up, making removal difficult. This large flat lizard was a popular food for early Native Americans.

The ample insect population consists of dune crawling circus beetles, moths, mesquite boring beetles, bees, ants, crickets, butterflies and several types of flies that area all irritatingly mean biters.

Scorpions and tarantulas also make their home in the deserts and canyons of Death Valley, and while they are not considered dangerous they are still a shocking sight to those not used to the unique beauty of these creatures. As with all wildlife, it is best to observe them from afar.

Possibly the most remarkable animal story in Death Valley is that of a fish. The pupfish, genus *Cyprinodon*, is thought to be related to fish that at one time lived in an ancient fresh-water lake called Lake Manly, which has long since dried up. Pupfish can still be found in small isolated water holes and streams after thousands of years of adapting to changes in their environment.

Right: Coyote, *Canis latrans*.
PHOTO BY JEFF FOOTT

for one of the few riparian communities within Death Valley National Park.

One of the most beautiful species growing on the upper desert slopes is the panamint daisy, *Enceliopsis argophylla grandiflora*. a lovely yellow flower indigenous to Death Valley. The Bristlecone pine, *Pinus aristata*, with its gnarled branches twisted by wind and freezing rain, resides far above the valley floor, is the oldest known living plant, with specimens known to be more than 4000 years old.

Right: Joshua tree at Lee Flat. The largest of the yuccas, Joshua trees were named by Mormon pioneers after the biblical leader.
PHOTO BY LARRY ULRICH

Above: The dark Ubehebe cinder fields contrast with the widely dispersed, light-colored desert bushes. Death Valley National Park.
PHOTO BY TOM DANIELSEN

The new additions to Death Valley National Park have added more than just 1.3 million acres to the boundaries of the park, it serves to

Above: A lone creosote bush atop a sand dune is back-lit by the full moon at dawn. Mesquite Flat, Death Valley National Park.
PHOTO BY JEFF GNASS

ensure that these unique wilderness environments, unlike any others on earth, are saved for the enjoyment of generations to come.

Right: Calthaleaf phacelia, desert sunflower and Death Valley gilmania.
PHOTO BY LARRY ULRICH

THE MINERS

Prospecting in Death Valley first became popular around 1850, although no one knows exactly when the first one-blanket prospector wandered into the region in search of the elusive mineral strike that was sure to bring fame and fortune. Most often, all that was found was solitude and hard work.

The first rush began in 1850, after pioneers following the Old Spanish Trail from Salt Lake City to San Bernardino claimed to have found gold nuggets at a place called Salt Spring. Small amounts of gold were indeed discovered at Salt Spring, but the expense of mining gold in such a remote location far exceeded the value of the small amounts of ore discovered.

Water, wood and affordable transportation were needed for successful mining operations, and were not readily found in Death Valley. Prospectors continued to flow into the area despite its lack of necessities, its inhospitable climate and harsh environment. Commonly, claims were filed by miners who believed that they had found ore rich mines, only to realize that the claims they had staked were not rich enough to pay the expensive price of doing business in the remote regions of Death Valley.

Success came to some of the lucky, and persistent, miners and stories of their strikes and new found wealth spurred on kindred souls despite the long odds against a major find.

One of the first modestly successful pocket miners in Death Valley was Tom Shaw who struck gold in the Gold Mountains in July 1866. He named his find the *State Line*. Unfortunately for Shaw, his claim never became the "monster load" he had originally believed it to be. Shaw kept returning to the Gold Mountains year after year in an attempt to make the *State Line* mine pay and his continued efforts paid off, on a smaller scale, once he purchased equipment to mill his own ore.

Another rush was taking place nearby, only this time silver was discovered. Just northwest of Gold Mountain lies Lida Spring and it was there two enterprising young men, William Black and William Scott, first discovered silver. They named their claim the *Cinderella* and soon other hopeful miners hit pay dirt with the *Lida Belle* and the *Brown's Hope* mines.

The silver boom near Lida Spring became the backbone of the small mining town of Lida. Created in May of 1872, Lida had the distinction of being the first mining town in Death Valley and was complete, including a saloon.

The discovery of borax by Aaron and Rosie Winters in 1880, launched what would prove to be Death Valley's most profitable mining period. The Harmony Borax Works, created in 1883, shipped well over one million pounds of borax each year until it closed in 1888 (see sidebar on page 29).

Legions of men searched for riches in Death Valley but very few were successful. Perhaps the most successful prospectors were those like Robert Bailey of Oroville, California, and Death Valley Scotty who always worked harder at searching for eager investors than they ever worked to find gold or silver.

"Bury me beside Jim Dayton in the valley we loved. Above me write:
Here lies Shorty Harris, a single blanket jackass prospector." Epitaph requested by Shorty (Frank) Harris, beloved gold hunter. 1856-1934.

Here Jas. Dayton, pioneer, perished, 1898.

To these trailmakers whose courage matched the dangers of the land, this bit of earth is dedicated forever.

National Park Service plaque commemorating two colorful Death Valley miners.

Preceding Pages: Wind patterns on sand dunes showing beetle and kangaroo rat tracks.
PHOTO BY JEFF FOOTT

Left: An abandoned mine entrance in Titus Canyon. Death Valley National Park, California.
PHOTO BY JEFF FOOTT

Right: These charcoal kilns in Wildrose Canyon were built in 1877 by George Hearst's Modock Consolidated Mining Company.
PHOTO BY LARRY ULRICH

THE MINERS CONTINUED...

The frenzied mining activity in Death Valley was undoubtedly more the result of wishful thinking and faulty facts than of that of actual success. The fortunes discovered in gold and silver mines of California's Sierra Nevada Mountains helped to draw hopeful miners from all over the country.

Rumors concerning a piece of silver, discovered by one of the lost '49ers, that was pure enough to be made into a gunsight, brought prospectors pouring into Death Valley during the 1850s. From then on miners scoured the mountains and valleys searching for the elusive *Lost Gunsight Lode* that never materialized.

Other stories about "lost" mines in Death Valley helped to fuel the mining frenzy. The most popular was the tale of Charles Breyfogle who claimed that a member of the surviving '49ers told him

Above: Lost Burro Mine in the Cottonwood Mountains.
PHOTO BY LARRY ULRICH

about a rich vein of gold ore spotted on a ledge somewhere near Death Valley. In the mid 1860s, Breyfogle found a grub-staker and, with a party of other prospectors, set off to find the place described to him. Although he never found the site, Breyfogle continued to search tirelessly year after year. Because of his sincere determination he had little trouble finding people optimistic enough to grubstake him in his continuing search for gold.

The expression "Breyfogling" was used for those unwilling to give up the search for Death Valley's "lost" mines. Stories of the *Lost Gunsight Lode* and *Breyfogle* mines continued to tantalize the never ending stream of prospectors who believed they had as good a chance as anyone in finding the fabled riches.

The life of a prospector was often

Below: The sunrises over *Skidoo*, once one of the most productive gold mines in Death Valley.
PHOTO BY TOM TILL

hard and dangerous and they faced serious perils at every turn. Prospectors had to be wary of everything from Indian attacks and claim jumpers to dehydration and snake bites. A man had to be tough in order to survive the hardships faced when working in Death Valley.

Although plenty of people lost money to nefarious prospectors, not all were as dishonest as the notorious Death Valley Scotty, who had more luck finding rich grubstakers than he ever had finding an actual mine. The average prospector had an honest desire to stake a claim that would make him richer than he had ever imagined, and most worked diligently, although often fruitlessly, to that end.

Finding a grubstake was the first hurdle for most prospectors to overcome in their search for riches. A grubstake was money provided by an investor in return for a percentage of any claims filed by the prospector during an agreed upon amount of time. The money was used to buy food, mules, picks, pans and the other supplies needed for the trip. The prospector led a solitary and itinerant lifestyle while he searched for riches. When he made a discovery of rocks containing gold, silver, copper or any other valuable substance he would head to

BORAX, THE WHITE GOLD...

The story of the first borax discovery in Death Valley is one of both hardship and luck, prime ingredients to many success stories.

Prospector Aaron Winters and his wife, Rosie, lived in a shack in Ash Meadows, east of Death Valley. Aaron had spent years searching in and around the valley for gold and silver, hoping to strike it rich.

One evening luck, in the form of a passing stranger, presented itself to the Winters. A man stopped at the Winters' ramshackle abode for the night and told the couple about fortunes being made in Nevada since the discovery of borax. The stranger showed them what borax looked like in both the raw form and after refinement. He also explained that sulfuric acid and alcohol were used to test borax and that if the combination of the chemicals and the suspected substance burned a bright green, then it was certainly borax.

Aaron Winters was fascinated with the subject and paid close attention to the descriptions of the chemicals and testing, knowing he had seen the same type of cotton ball crystals lying on the floor of Death Valley.

The next day, after the traveler went on his way, Aaron and Rosie left their shack to search for the chemicals they needed to test for borax.

It took only a few days to collect the necessary materials and set up camp on the floor of Death Valley at Furnace Creek, not far from the crystal cotton balls they'd be testing. Aaron anxiously lit the concoction and exclaim in jubilation, "She burns green, Rosie! We're rich, by God!"

The Winters were able to sell their secret location to W. T. Coleman and F. M. Smith, major players in the booming borax business, for $20,000. The Winter's bought a ranch in Nevada with the proceeds of the sale and left Death Valley in 1881.

The discovery of borax, a crystalline compound of boron that occurs as a mineral, in Death Valley proved to be one of the most profitable mining endeavors in Death Valley.

Borax was first discovered in the US in 1856, by Dr. John Veatch, with other discoveries soon to follow. Until borax was first discovered in America it came from as far away as Italy, Peru, Chile and Turkey. Consequently the cost was very inflated.

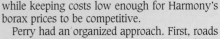

"Borax King," Francis Marion Smith.
PHOTO COURTESY OF US BORAX & CHEMICAL CORPORATION.

William Troup discovered ulexite, or cotton ball borax, at Columbus Marsh and Salt Wells, Nevada, in 1871. Francis Marion Smith, later known as "Borax" Smith, filed his first claim in October of 1872, in Columbus, Nevada. In 1873, brothers John and Dennis Searles discovered borax at what is today Searles Lake but was originally known as Borax Lake.

William Tell Coleman was a borax distributor for both Dr. Veatch and William Troup by the time the Smith Brothers arrived on the scene. Later, Coleman and Francis M. Smith worked together with Julius Smith producing large quantities of borax. Coleman acted as a sales agent, distributor and sometimes financial backer. Coleman had a borax refinery in Alameda, California, where Frank and his brother Julius Smith sent their borax for final processing.

In 1880 Frank Smith, expanding his operations, bought the Pacific Borax Company and in 1882 he and Coleman began to develop the Winters claim at Furnace Creek, naming the site Harmony Borax Works. While a lot of hard work went into building the refinery at Harmony, the biggest job was devising an easy and inexpensive way to get the borax from Furnace Creek to the town of Mohave, over 165 miles southwest of Death Valley.

J. W. S. Perry, then a superintendent at Harmony, was the man who solved the transportation problem, designing wagons able to make the 300 mile round trip over desert and mountains

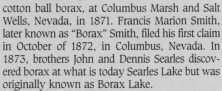

Left: The Harmony Borax Works, founded by Frank "Borax" Smith in 1882, was abandoned in 1888.
PHOTO BY JEFF FOOTT

while keeping costs low enough for Harmony's borax prices to be competitive.

Perry had an organized approach. First, roads dependable enough to carry enormous loads the mammoth wagons would haul were constructed. Existing roads had to be improved and extended. He did this with the help of Chinese laborers who toiled in the harsh valley environment and used sledgehammers on a section of road crossing the Devil's Golf Course, a salt bed made up of sharply pointed salt pinnacles several feet deep.

To carry the mammoth loads of borax, Perry commissioned construction of the famous 20 mule team wagons that remain synonymous with Borax to this day (see sidebar page 30).

Although Harmony was the largest producer in Death Valley it wasn't the only one. Eagle Borax Works, owned by Frenchman Isadore Daunet, was built in the winter of 1882-1883 just a couple of miles north of Bennetts Well. Eagle Borax Works produced as much as 22 tons of concentrated borax a month.

Unfortunately, Daunet's equipment would not perform in the intense heat of the summer, forcing him to close until cooler weather. When he was able to resume processing the price of borax had dropped to 10¢ a pound. In less than a year he was facing bankruptcy. Daunet's life took another downturn as his new wife, realizing that her husband was soon to be penniless, left and filed for a divorce. Daunet ended his problems, and his life, by putting a gun to his head and pulling the trigger.

Old Dinah, a steam engine built to replace the 20 mule teams.
COURTESY US BORAX & CHEMICAL CORP AND HENRY E. HUNTINGTON LIBRARY

Harmony Borax Works closed in 1888. Shortly thereafter Borax Smith acquired several holdings previously controlled by W.T. Coleman. When Smith took the reins from Coleman he went from being called Borax Smith to the "Borax King."

Smiths' greatest strength was his willingness to take risks to realize business potential. His biggest weakness was his inability to procure long term financing. Because of his short term borrowing, he was forced out of the borax business in 1914, shortly before his 68th birthday. Unlike Coleman, he made a dramatic return to the borax business at the age of 75 and regained his fortune.

town to have his find assayed. If the sample proved to be valuable, he would often look for the busiest place in a mining town, the saloon.

The boom towns in Death Valley were as dangerous as any of their time. The wild, often lawless, towns were filled with thugs who would cheat a man at poker and then kill him in a gunfight when they were accused of being a four-flusher. Many miners struck it rich one day, only to lose everything in a poker game the next day. A miner's life was never easy.

Left: Rylolite, in the Bullfrog Hills east of Death Valley, once had almost 8,000 citizens. When the gold ran out in 1911, the town went bust.
PHOTO BY LARRY ULRICH

The ebb and flow of mining in Death Valley continued and even George Hearst, Comstock Lode tycoon and father of William Randolph Hearst of Hearst Castle, got into the act.

George Hearst purchased a mining claim in the Lookout district of Wildrose Canyon that was originally discovered by Jerome Childs. He created the Modock Consolidated Mining Company and began production of silver-lead bullion. In order to keep the furnaces burning, the Modock Company built ten charcoal kilns that yielded approximately 2000 bushels of charcoal a week. The charcoal kilns, built in 1877, are still standing in excellent condition in Wildrose Canyon today.

20 MULE TEAMS AND BORAX PROCESSING...

With the discovery of Borax in Death Valley came the arduous task of transporting and processing the mineral into a form that could be used commercially.

The job of arranging transportation of borax at Harmony Borax Works fell to J. W. S. Perry, who met the challenge with alacrity. After building new roads and repairing existing roads over the 165 mile route from Furnace Creek southwest to the town of Mojave, he went on to design wagons that would be able to haul loads of well over ten tons. The wagon beds measured 16 feet long, 4 feet wide and 6 feet deep. The front wheels were 5 feet in diameter and the rear wheels were 7 feet in diameter. There was an iron tire on each wheel that was 1 inch thick by 8 inches wide. Perry ordered 10 wagons from a company in Mohave at a price of $900 each.

Perry's next job was to divide the route into sections representing an average daily journey, approximately 15 to 20 miles apart, depending upon whether the team was coming in empty or going out full. Shelters were built at the chosen sites for the team to use on their 20 day, 300 mile, round trip journey. These shelters, or stations, were, due to necessity, built near available springs. Those shelters that were dry had water brought to them by tank wagons that were hauled back and forth to the springs.

Each wagon team consisted of two wagons pulled by a 20 mule team, actually consisting of 18 mules and two horses, and driven by an experienced driver and his assistant, or swamper. Swamper duties included manning the brakes on the rear wagon during steep descents as well as cooking and generally assisting with the care of the animals and wagons.

It should be noted that Perry's wagons withstood the less than smooth roads with great strength and endurance. For the most part, only the wheels had to be repaired or replaced with any regularity during the five years they were in use at the Harmony Borax Works. While the wagons could take a beating all year long, the animals and humans could only tolerate so much. Shipments of borax were halted during the months of June through September since neither the animals nor the humans could endure the

20 Mule Team Wagons were used by Harmony Borax Works to haul Borax in the 1880s.
PHOTO: TOM TILL

extreme heat of Death Valley in the summer.

In 1904, a new mule team was trained and a couple of the old wagons were brought out of retirement for an appearance at the St. Louis Exposition. The 20 mule team was an instant success and Pacific Coast Borax Company sent the team on a tour of the eastern United States. The mule teams went from state to state handing out free product samples and generating plenty of free publicity for the company.

Ironically, it was long after the 1888 closure of the Harmony Borax Works that the 20 mule team became a trademark for the Pacific Coast Borax Company.

The 20 Mule Team advertising campaign was used by the Pacific Coast Borax Company during the popular *Death Valley Days* radio show in the 1930s and continued during the television series in the 1950s. These shows, written by Ruth Cornwall Woodman, featured glorified accounts of Death Valley's early days and created national interest in the Valley.

It is hard to imagine modern life without borax since borax, along with other components in the boron group, can be found in many of the

products we use every day. Borates make glass shiny and strong and are used in bottles, optical lenses, and headlight lenses. Fiberglass on cars, boats and planes is stronger because of borates and porcelain enamels used on appliances, including refrigerators and washing machines, shines brighter and is crack resistant because of the borates used in their finish.

Borons, or derivatives of boron, are also used in weed killers, building materials, mouthwash, glues, lotions, detergents, antifreeze, make-up, paints, paper and soaps. Borax may be most commonly known in the United States in the form of laundry detergent.

Refining borax involved separating the borax from other chemicals by dissolving it in hot water. The liquid was left to cool for up to 10 days, with insoluble waste drained off at regular intervals. A crystallized form of borax remained.

Below: 20 Mule Team Canyon. Death Valley and Amargosa deposits produced about two million pounds of borax per year, doubling the borax production in America.
PHOTO: TOM TILL

Panamint City, northeast of Ballarat, was founded shortly after the *Wonder of the World, Challenge, Stewart's Wonder, Wyoming, Hemlock* and *Wonder Gulch* silver mines were staked in 1873, by a band of criminals hiding out from the law. The mines were sold to Nevada Senators William M. Stewart and John P. Jones, with Stewart arranging a deal between the criminals and their victim, Wells Fargo Bank, which allowed them to return the stolen money in exchange for their freedom.

It was the discovery of the *Keane Wonder Mine* in 1904, by two prospectors, Jack Keane and Domingo Etcharren, that kicked off the Bullfrog gold rush. The *Keane Wonder,* located in the Funeral Mountains, was one of the more successful Death Valley gold mines, turning out approximately $250,000 in gold each year. It

Above: The ruins of *The Keane Wonder Mill* in the Funeral Mountains of Death Valley, one of the most successful gold mines in the region.
PHOTO: JEFF GNASS

finally closed down in August of 1912, only three months after being sold to a group of rich Philadelphians.

The *Skidoo* mine was another successful venture. John Thompson and John Ramsey staked several claims near Emigrant Canyon. They sold out to Bob Montgomery, a miner who had made a fortune at Bullfrog. It is said that Montgomery's wife was the person who gave the mining venture its whimsical name.

Gold, silver and copper were the minerals sought after by early prospectors, and while many men made and kept their fortunes, most never realized their dreams of striking it rich. The discovery of borax proved to be the most profitable mining ventures and many made

Following Pages: Salt Creek in Death Valley.
PHOTO: JEFF GNASS

small fortunes selling their claims to the Pacific Borax Company.

Mining continued in Death Valley until 1976, when Congress passed the Mining in the Parks Act, which prohibited filing of future mining claims and began eliminating existing mines.

Right: The ruins at Ashford Mill.
PHOTO BY JEFF GNASS

FURNACE CREEK...

Long before the arrival of the first white man, Furnace Creek was known as Tumbisha, or Coyote Rock, by the Shoshone and Paiute Indians who lived in the area. When the first white men struggled through the valley the Indians observed their plight from afar, seldom interfering as if somehow knowing the valley itself would protect their privacy.

When the 49ers were lost and stranded while attempting to cross the Valley in 1849, on their way to the Goldfields of northern California, they set up a camp along Furnace Creek Wash. They awaited rescue by William Lewis Manly and John Rogers who hiked 200 miles to Los Angeles, and back, in a dramatic rescue.

Several years later a prospector by the name of Dr. Darwin French, upon the discovery of a small furnace along its bank, gave the creek its name. A plentiful supply of water from the Travertine and Texas Springs along the Furnace Creek Wash made the area a virtual oasis in the middle of the hottest place in the continental United States.

In the mid-1870s an enterprising man named Andy Laswell, realized the potential in providing horse feed to miners at Panamint City and used the water resource to grow alfalfa. When the Panamint mine began to falter, Andy Laswell abandoned his ranch and moved on.

Rudolph Neuschwander, under the direction of W. T. Coleman of the Harmony Borax Works, created the Greenland Ranch. Neuschwander installed an irrigation ditch running a mile from Furnace Creek to provide water for 40 acres of alfalfa grown to feed mules and horses owned by the borax works. Fruit trees and a vegetable garden were also planted as a supplement to the outside food supply.

Although Harmony Borax Works closed the same year that Borax Smith took control, the Greenland Ranch continued to be maintained by caretaker James Dayton.

The ranch, which would later became known as the Furnace Creek Ranch, was kept up well enough over the years to begin production of vegetables, fruits and animal feed for the miners who came to work the new borax interests in both Death Valley Junction and Ryan in the early 1900s.

As tourism became a serious source of income in Death Valley in the mid-1920s, the Pacific Coast Borax Company decided to build a hotel in the valley.

Architect Albert C. Martin of Los Angeles was selected to draw the plans and in the fall of 1926 construction began. The Furnace Creek Inn was built just above sea level, on a ridge above Furnace Creek Wash.

The two story, mission-style building with its stucco exterior opened in February of 1927, although additions were made to the Inn over the years until its completion in 1940. The Inn gained a reputation as a viable retreat in the desert as the years went by and Death Valley became a national monument in 1933.

In 1956, Fred Harvey, Inc., a leader in the hospitality industry, took over management of the Furnace Creek Inn. In 1969, Fred Harvey purchased the Furnace Creek Inn and Ranch Resort from the U.S. Borax Company. The company continues today to provide excellent accommodations, with the emphasis on service and attention to detail the company has long been known for, to the visitors of Death Valley.

Furnace Creek Resort offers many fascinating historic artifacts for the Death Valley visitor to discover. A pair of the original 20 Mule Team wagons sits at the entrance to Furnace Creek Ranch across from the steam engine, dubbed Old Dinah, that was purchased by Borax Smith in 1894, to replace the 20 mule teams working the Borate mine near Daggett.

The Borax Museum, located on the Furnace Creek property, allows visitors to see equipment used for mining borax. One fascinating exhibit is the extensive mineral collection contributed by Harry P. Gower which shows examples of borax in its many different forms. Also on view are many historical photographs of the area's mines, the 20 mule teams and the miners.

Below: Furnace Creek Inn with the Funeral Mountains in the background.
PHOTO BY TOM BEAN

DEATH VALLEY SCOTTY

Walter Scott was probably the most famous prospector ever to come out of Death Valley, an incredible feat for someone who never actually did any mining.

Born in Kentucky in 1872, the youngest child born to George and Anna Scott, Walter spent only a short time in the blue grass state. Anna died soon after Scotty was born and George, a horse trainer, remarried a short time later.

Scotty's stepmother felt the boy would benefit more from school than traveling the harness-racing circuit with his father. Scotty wasn't interested in school and decided at an early age to follow his older brothers west.

He worked at several odd jobs while still in his teens, including one with a survey crew running a state boundary line between Nevada and California, bringing him to Death Valley for the first time. He later worked in Death Valley for the Harmony Borax Works as a swamper, or water boy, on one of the twenty-mule team wagons.

When Scotty was about 18 years old a scout for the Buffalo Bill Wild West Show witnessed his skill at handling horses and hired him to perform with the show. Scotty spent twelve years with the show, touring the United States and Europe. By close observation of "Major" John Burke, the publicist who helped create the legend of Buffalo Bill, Scotty learned the arts of grandiose exaggeration and self promotion. Lessons that would come in handy.

Scotty's career with the show came to an end, for reasons still somewhat of a mystery due to Scotty's propensity to tell tales, in 1902. He went on to become more famous than perhaps even he could have imagined.

Shortly before leaving the Wild West Show, Scotty met and married a young widow. Ella Josephine Milius was working in a candy store in New York City when Scotty sweet talked the 24 year-old into a quick trip to the alter. Scotty and "Jack," his nickname for her, were married in a Cincinnati courthouse November 5, 1900.

Facing unemployment and starvation for both himself and his new wife, Scotty had to depend upon his wits to steer him in his next career move. Armed with several months of experience in working mines in Colorado, and a couple of gold samples that belonged to Jack, Scotty went looking for his first grubstake.

Never one to miss an opportunity, Scotty remembered meeting Julian Gerard, a wealthy executive of the Knickerbocker Trust Company. Gerard had once made a general invitation to several members of the Buffalo Bill Show to look him up if they were ever in New York. Jack's pieces of gold ore and Scotty's enthusiasm for the mine he claimed to have found in Death Valley, sold Gerard on the idea. Scotty left town with $1500 advanced by Gerard.

Over the next few years Scotty received thousands of dollars from Gerard, and quite probably, several other grubstakers. He used the success of the Tonopah and Goldfield rush to feed the rumors of his own successes.

Scotty carefully planned and directed a series of events that brought him into the national

Left: A weather vane depicting Scotty's likeness with blue skies above and dark clouds on the horizon, a metaphor for Scotty's life.
PHOTO BY JEFF FOOTT

Right: The Chimes Tower at Scotty's Castle, Death Valley National Park, California.
PHOTO BY JEFF FOOTT

spotlight. The first maneuver was the apparent "theft" of $12,000 worth of gold dust on a train between Pittsburgh and Philadelphia. Scotty was reported to have remarked quite calmly, "There's plenty more where that came from," shortly after reporting the theft.

The story of the gold theft and the cavalier prospector made front page news across the country.

Scotty, knowing the world was watching, went off on a conspicuous spending spree. With the help of a cunning reporter Scotty's excessive tips and flamboyant show of cash, especially big bills, were brought to the attention of the world. The showmanship Scotty learned during his Wild West Show days played an important

Walter Scott.
PHOTO BY STACY

part in the success of his ploys.

Scotty's investors read the papers, along with the rest of the American public, and believed that he really had hit pay dirt... and that he was holding out on them. Gerard made several attempts to force Scotty to show him the mines but was thwarted by one excuse after another.

Scotty was on his way to pulling off his most ambitious publicity stunt ever, "The Coyote Special." An inspired promoter from Los Angeles, E. Burdon Gaylord, saw the dashing Scotty, in his trademark blue pants, blue or white shirt and bright red tie, as the perfect vehicle to promote prospective mining properties located near Death Valley. His idea would put Scotty in the news papers once again.

Gaylord had Scotty pay $5,500, with money

provided by Gaylord, to the Santa Fe Railroad Company for the simple purpose of setting a new record time for the trip from Los Angeles

Above: Cracked mud and sand dunes in Death Valley.
PHOTO BY DICK DIETRICH

to Chicago. Scotty would make a few bucks on the deal while gaining more notoriety and adoration from the public, all while having a good time. Scotty insisted a dining car filled with only the best food and alcohol be included, since he always liked to go in style.

On July 9, 1905, the "Coyote Special" left Los Angeles at one o'clock in the afternoon. The train carried Scotty, "Jack," two reporters and a dog. People across America followed the progress of the speeding train. Crowds lined the tracks at stations along the way, cheering the train as it passed. The trip ended in a record breaking 44 hours and 54 minutes, a record that held for 30 years, until the diesel engine was brought into use.

When the excitement died down enough for cynics to suggest the special train trip was probably concocted by the Santa Fe Railroad as a publicity stunt, the railroad issued a public statement denying any involvement in such a scheme and insisted they were simply supplying a fast train for a well paying customer.

At the time of Scotty's wild train ride he had been partners with Albert Johnson for almost a year. Their meeting, in late 1904, would be the beginning of a long and, at least for Scotty, prosperous relationship.

In 1906 Johnson arrived in Death Valley for the first time. His intention to see the mines his money had supported never materialized. Scott led him on a tour of Death Valley that never quite took him to the so-called mines. Johnson was an unsuspecting witness to the charade at Wingate Pass and even played a part by helping Scotty's brother, Warner, when he was injured in the phony fray.

While most people would have been furious at such a ruse, Johnson was not. It seems his experience in Death Valley with the legendary Death Valley Scotty was to be one of the most exciting periods of his life.

THE BATTLE OF WINGATE PASS ...

An unsuccessful scheme concocted by Scotty, later to be known as "The Battle of Wingate Pass" began with a desire to fleece investors of their money and ended, years later, with Scotty's public humiliation.

Scotty was approached by A.Y. Pearl, a mining promoter interested in investing in Scotty's famous mine. Scotty showed serious interested in doing business with Pearl but Scotty had a problem when investors demanded to inspect the mine before investing any money, for Scotty had no mine.

Scotty, never one to pass up an opportunity, agreed to take the group, which included Albert Johnson, one of Scotty's more generous grubstakers, into Death Valley. Scotty decided to stage a phony shoot out before the group ever reached his "mine." The idea was to scare off the investors while leaving them with the impression that his mine must be worth plenty if outlaws were willing to kill for it. The party included A.Y. Pearl, an expert mining engineer named Daniel Owen and two of Scotty's brothers, Bill and Warner. There were also a couple of other men to "help" out on the trip.

On February 26, 1906, as the party traveled through Wingate Pass, Scotty's men were sent ahead to set the scene. Evening was almost upon the party when bullets started to fly and all hell broke loose. Scotty lost his cool when his brother Warner was wounded and he began yelling "Stop the shooting!" A pretty surprising reaction from a man with a reputation of being a sure shot who always hit what he aimed at.

Luckily, Johnson had a fully equipped medical bag and patched Warner's groin wound well enough to enable him to reach a doctor.

Once again Scotty made headlines, but this time it was on charges of assault with a deadly weapon. His plan to fool the investors came to light and the media had a field day maligning the same man they had recently admired.

Just before the trial was to begin the charges

were dropped due to a jurisdictional dispute. It seems the crimes were committed in Inyo County and not San Bernardino County. Inyo County chose not to pursue the case and all defendants were quickly released.

Scotty still wasn't out of trouble. A $152,000 damage suit was filed by his brother, Warner. Scotty promised to pay Warner's medical bills if he would drop the charges. Warner agreed and everyone was happy, except for the doctor who was never paid the $1,001.25 for Warner's treatment Scotty had agreed to pay.

Six years later, that same unpaid doctor saw the headlines proclaiming Scotty a millionaire after the sale of his mine in Death Valley. The doctor sued for payment of the long delinquent medical bill.

Scotty was forced to admit in a court of law that he was a liar who'd never really had a mine. He revealed that even the much publicized train ride, one of his greatest publicity stunts, was paid for by someone else and that he had been living off grubstaking money he had received from both Albert Johnson and Julian Gerard throughout the years.

After the trial Scotty returned to Death Valley in disgrace. Not much was heard of him until Albert Johnson began building a castle in the desert some 13 years later. The castle brought fame back to Scotty.

Death Valley Scotty and Albert Johnson, two men who shared a life-long love of Death Valley.
NATIONAL PARK SERVICE

Scotty avoided much of the furor surrounding the Wingate debacle by leaving for Seattle, Washington, to star in a play called "Scotty, King of the Desert Mine." The play was written by an opportunistic playwright, Charles A. Taylor, and was loosely based on Scotty's escapades. Unfortunately, Taylor had to post bail for his star when Scotty was arrested in both San Francisco and Los Angeles. Charged with assault with a deadly weapon for his part in the episode at Wingate Pass.

The Wingate Pass episode eventually passed with no real impact on Scotty. Eventually all charges were dropped. Scotty was able to talk his brother out of a $152,000 lawsuit and the excitement came to an end...until six years later (see sidebar). The Battle of Wingate Pass reappeared in the news announcing that Death Valley Scotty was a self promoting braggart and a fraud. They seemed

Death Valley Scotty.
ASSOCIATED PRESS PHOTO

to enjoy tearing down the man they had so many times portrayed as a national hero.

This was a low point in the life of Walter Scott and he headed for his own personal retreat, Death Valley. Albert Johnson always believed in Scotty, although he may have been forced to acknowledge that Scotty was never going to produce an ore rich mine, but Johnson knew Scotty as a wonderful and entertaining friend. A friend worth keeping, no matter what the cost.

Johnson began his regular visits to Death Valley in 1909, several years before Scotty's public confession of fraud, and during the time he spent with Scotty he came to know the man better than almost anyone. Although Scotty was a boastful man and a confessed fraud he must have had many good qualities for a man of Johnson's moral background to become his greatest friend. Bessie Johnson also became close to Scotty, another testimony to Scotty's better qualities.

Many stories are told about Scotty's kindness to animals, lost strangers and all underdogs. One story tells of how Scotty, outraged because a Chinese laborer was not allowed to eat in any dining room in Rhyolite, Nevada, chose to share a meal with the man in the middle of the street rather than eat in a place that wouldn't serve a hungry man.

There is no doubt about Scotty's skills as an outdoorsman, he and Albert Johnson trekked all through Death Valley, with Scotty setting up camp, hunting, cooking and watching out for the tenderfooted Easterner.

During the years that followed Scotty's humiliating trial, Johnson took care of Scotty by sending a small sum every month to keep him fed and to address his other needs. Johnson also sent money to Scotty's wife. Later, when Jack sued Scotty for support, Johnson built a house for her and Scotty's son, Walter Perry Scott, and continued sending her money. Scotty was never accused of being a good husband or father, he and his family spent years apart, with Scotty barely mentioning either his wife or his son.

Scotty had been out of the limelight for several years, until 1922, when Johnson began the construction on what would eventually become Scotty's Castle. When construction began, so did Scotty's habit of telling tales. People believed the buildings were financed by Scotty's secret mine. Scotty fed the rumors and claimed to have spent a half a million dollars on construction.

Johnson allowed, and possibly even abetted,

Above: A salted pool at Badwater reflects Telescope Peak.
PHOTO BY JACK W. DYKINGA

Scotty's tales by implying that he was simply a banker from Chicago who worked for Mr. Scott. The Castle became an extension of both men and their initials are scattered all over the property as evidence of their friendship.

Death Valley Scotty's most successful find was a special friendship with Albert and Bessie Johnson which lasted for over 40 years.

THE WIVES, BESSIE AND JACK...

Not much is known about the relationship between Walter Scott and his wife Jack. We do know that although they had a son, they spent very little time together.

Jack's maiden name was Ella Josephine Milius. She was working in a candy shop in New York when she met Scott in the spring

Jack Scott in 1937.
VAN DYKE STUDIOS

of 1900. Scotty was taken by Jack's personality and style and convinced the 24 year old widow to marry him. After only months of courting, Scotty and Jack married.

Jack and Scott would spend very little time living together during their married life. Scotty set her up in a small apartment in Los Angeles before heading off to spend his grubstake money. Jack and Scotty were together again for the Santa Fe train ride that brought Scotty so much attention, but after that they rarely ever spent time together.

The relationship between Albert and Bessie Johnson was the opposite. They were always very close. Albert met Bessie Morris Penniman while attending Cornell University and they married in 1896.

Bessie and Albert were alike in many ways. They were both quiet, very conservative and intensely religious people who believed in doing God's work. Bessie often preached at revival meetings. Later, during the construction of the Castle, if Bessie was home all of the workers,

with the exception of the Indians, were required to attend her Sunday sermons.

After Albert Johnson's earliest trips to Death Valley, he brought his wife with him and she was to share his enthusiasm for the area. It was Bessie that influenced Albert's decision to build a home in Death Valley. He and Bessie spent long hours working with the architect and the various craftsmen selected to construct their Death Valley Ranch.

While Scotty didn't spend much time with Jack, he did spend time with Bessie and they formed a strong friendship. Ironically, it was Johnson who supported Jack for many years, since she had little luck in cornering Scotty. Even her lawyers attempts to make Scotty send her support failed. Albert sent Jack money and eventually built her a home.

Bessie Johnson was killed in an automobile accident near Towne Pass in the Panamint Range on April 22, 1943. Albert lived on for another five years and died on January 7, 1948, at the age of 76, from an exploratory operation.

Scotty died at age 82 on January 5, 1954. He was mourned by many but neither Jack, nor his son, was present at his funeral. He was buried alongside of his dog Windy near the castle.

Scotty, Bessie, and Albert.
NPS PHOTO

SCOTTY'S CASTLE

Hidden deep in a remote canyon at the northern confines of Death Valley sits an extraordinary vision, Scotty's Castle. The Spanish-style mansion, originally named Death Valley Ranch, has captivated visitors with its colorful history since its inception.

The story of Scotty's Castle began long before its foundation was laid and involves two men, Walter Scott, a prospector and sometimes con man, and Albert M. Johnson, a Chicago millionaire and devout Christian.

The two men met in late 1904 when Scott went to Chicago with the intention of finding an investor to grubstake his expeditions into Death Valley. A grubstake was an agreement between a prospector and an investor who would advance the prospector cash in exchange for a percentage of any claims made by the prospector within a specified amount of time, or, until the money ran out. If, at the end of the contracted time, the prospector had found no ore the agreement either expired or was reinstated with another chunk of money.

That November, Albert Johnson and Edward Shedd agreed to give Scott and his temporary partner, Obadiah Sands, a stake of $2,500 in exchange for a two-thirds share of any claims filed by Scott and Sands before January 6, 1906.

Even though the venture failed due to the nefarious behavior of Scott, who spent the money on good times and self promotion, Johnson believed that Scott had discovered, or had the ability to discover, ore rich mines in Death Valley. It was this belief that led Johnson to stake Scott almost $23,000, a small fortune in the early 1900s, in another venture.

In 1906 Johnson arrived in Death Valley for the first time. His intention to see the mines his money had supported never materialized. Scott led him on a tour of Death Valley that never quite took him to the so-called mines.

While most people would have been furious at such a ruse, Johnson was not. His experience in Death Valley was filled with excitement and adventure. His trip began as a part of Scotty's charade, but he developed an appreciation for Death Valley's rugged beauty.

The desert air seemed to revitalize Johnson, whose health had been poor ever since the 1899 train wreck that had killed his father and broken his back, causing Albert to endure years of convalescing. He became very fond of the tall tales and good cooking so generously served up by the one and only Death Valley Scotty. Far from being disappointed, he had a wonderful time traipsing around the valley.

Johnson returned year after year to explore Death Valley with Scotty and experience once again the place that made him feel so alive. After his first few visits he brought with him his beloved wife, Bessie. It was during a stay at their favorite campsite in Grapevine Canyon that Bessie remarked that they should build a real house to stay in during their winter visits. Bessie was not fond of the snakes and insects that often invaded their tents.

So began the Johnson's life long friendship with both Death Valley and Walter Scott.

Left: A fall morning shines on Scotty's Castle, nestled in Grapevine Canyon. Death Valley National Park, California.
PHOTO BY JEFF GNASS

Right: A detail of the ironwork in an entrance gate at Scotty's Castle. The initials, J and S, are found throughout the Castle and Death Valley Ranch lands and represent Albert Johnson and Walter Scott, lifelong friends.
PHOTO BY JEFF FOOTT

In 1915, Albert Johnson began purchasing the available mining claims and homesteads in the Grapevine Canyon area. His purchases included the holdings of German immigrant Jacob Steininger, who grew vegetables and fruits on his spring-fed ranch. It took 12 years for Johnson to purchase over fifteen hundred acres of land in and around the canyon.

Grapevine Canyon was an ideal location for the Johnson's to build a home. An elevation of 3000 feet above sea level, or 3282 feet above the lowest point in Death Valley, results in cooler temperatures in the canyon. Grapevine Canyon is tucked into the folds of a mountain on the northern end of Death Valley and is protected from the more serious desert sand storms while admitting cooling winds. The canyon also provides a steady source of the most important resource found in the desert, water.

Construction of three rectangular stucco buildings began in the fall of 1922. In short order the main building, measuring 32 feet by 96 feet, was completed. This building contained living quarters for the Johnson's, a guest room on the upper level, a kitchen, storage room and an apartment for Scotty downstairs. The second building served as a garage and workshop, and the third, a much smaller building, eventually was to become the cook house.

During construction renewed speculation about Scotty began. Had he finally struck it

rich? Was he paying for the buildings with money from a new secret mine? After years of being out of the public eye, Scotty saw the perfect opportunity to renew the almost forgotten Death Valley Scotty legend. Scotty often referred to the project as his "castle" or his "shack" and the name "Scotty's Castle" has obviously struck the fancy of the American public because that's what it has been called right from the start. Albert Johnson seemed to encourage Scotty's exaggerations and enjoyed the intrigue surrounding the project.

While the first buildings had all the modern conveniences available in the 1920s, they were very plain in appearance. Johnson, influenced perhaps by all of the attention and intrigue surrounding Scotty and "his" castle, decided to enlarge and embellish his property to a more castle-like appearance.

Johnson first enlisted the help of prominent architect Frank Lloyd Wright. While the ideas put forth by Wright were indeed interesting, he envisioned an adobe Indian village, Johnson preferred a Spanish-style hacienda. He turned next to an old college chum of Bessie's, Matt Roy Thompson. Bessie had attended Stanford University with Thompson before transferring to Cornell University and over the years they had maintained their friendship. Thompson sketched plans converting the plain rectangular buildings using a series of arches, architecture similar to that found at Stanford.

Charles Alexander MacNeilledge, a trusted designer who had worked on both Johnson's Chicago home and his office was hired next. MacNeilledge was brought in to direct planning of the Castle and to assist Thompson in all areas of the project.

Dewey Kruckeburg, a landscape architect, was hired to beautify the grounds with plants

ALBERT M. JOHNSON...

Albert M. Johnson was a serious young man of 32 when he first met Death Valley Scotty. Their friendship lasted over 40 years.

Born the son of a rich Ohio businessman in 1872, Johnson's family businesses included banking and utilities and upon graduation from Cornell University he entered the family business. While attending Cornell University Johnson met Bessie Morris Penniman, a devoted Christian woman from Walnut Creek, California. In 1896, they were married.

The Johnson's were deeply religious people who did not believe in the use of tobacco, bad language or alcohol and instead were fond of good old fashioned revival meetings.

In 1899 tragedy struck the Johnson family in the form of a train wreck. Johnson and his father were in Colorado, checking out business prospects, when the train they were riding on derailed. An oncoming train, unaware of the accident ahead, plowed straight into the rear of the derailed train, breaking Johnson's back and killing his father.

After eighteen months of painful hospitalization, Johnson was well enough to go home to recover from the accident. Johnson lived with the pain he received from his injuries for the rest of his life. Albert was forced to adapt to a physically easier job and consequently became partners with E. A. Shedd in a real estate investment business in Chicago. Johnson and Shedd invested in a deal that purchased the National Life Insurance Company.

Albert Johnson involved himself in running National Life and in 1926, became Chairman of the Board and controller of 90 percent of the stock. Albert's earnings skyrocketed to approximately one million dollars a year, high even by today's standards, it was an incredible fortune during the 1920s.

Johnson, an engineering major in college, had always been fascinated in mining and Scotty was only one of the prospectors he had staked over the years. In 1906, Albert arrived in Death Valley for the first time. He and his partner had

Albert M. Johnson.
PHOTO BY STACY

been sending money to Scotty for long enough. They wanted to see the mines Scotty had claimed to have discovered. Scotty, having no mines to show, then invented what came to be known as the "Battle of Wingate Pass," an ambush staged by Scotty that was intended to scare his partners right out of Death Valley.

While most people would have been furious at such a ruse, Johnson was not. It seems that Johnson's experience in Death Valley with the legendary Death Valley Scotty was one of the most exciting periods in his life. Johnson enjoyed Scotty's antics and was at times drawn into an easy banter with Scotty in which he added to the audacious Scotty's tales with his own sly wit.

An added bonus to visiting Death Valley was the way the clear desert air seemed to revitalize Johnson. He returned year after year to the desert and the company of his crafty friend, Death Valley Scotty.

Although the Stock Market Crash and the Great Depression severely affected Johnson's wealth, he never went broke. He and his wife lived comfortably in Hollywood, California and continued to spend time at the Castle until their deaths in the 1940s. Scotty stayed at the Castle until his death in 1954.

The Gospel Foundation of California was created by Albert Johnson for the sole purpose of administering his estate after his death. He made arrangements for his friend Scotty to live the remainder of his life in the castle following Johnson's death in 1948. The foundation continued the operation of Scotty's Castle until it was purchased in 1970 for $850,000 by the National Park Service.

Above: A weather vane perched atop the Main House depicts Scotty cooking over a campfire. The subtle detail of the vane and the quality of its craftsmanship is typical of Albert and Bessie Johnson's attention to detail.
PHOTO BY JEFF FOOTT

and trees suitable to the buildings design.

Another important participant in the transformation of the Castle was Martin de Dubovay, who was a highly skilled Hungarian architect with experience in both South American and European architecture. He was well-known for his detail work and his skills in this area assisted MacNeilledge in the design of the wrought-iron fixtures, wood carvings, and tile patterns used in the Castle.

The difficulties facing the crew were daunting but Johnson had chosen his location wisely. The Bullfrog Goldfield Railroad, serviced by the Tonopah and Tidewater Railroad was only 20 miles away. The railroad delivered freight cars filled with tons of building supplies. Nails, bolts, bundles of wire, lumber, tile, bags of plaster and mortar were just a few of the supplies delivered at Bonnie Claire before being trucked the final twenty miles to the Castle.

A never ending supply of sand and gravel was right in their back yard. Death Valley has been called "the biggest gravel pit in the world" and all that was necessary was to construct a gravel separator to supply all the sand and gravel needed for the project.

The closing of the Railroad in 1928 was a serious blow to the construction effort. When Johnson and his crew became aware of the imminent closure they immediately stockpiled building materials before discontinuation of the rail service would result in costly shipments by truck from Los Angeles or Beatty, Nevada.

A basement was dug below the main house with tunnels extending to many of the other buildings including the Powerhouse and the Gas Tank House. This allowed easier installation and access to electrical, sewer and water lines. The walls of the two story building were reinforced by the addition of stronger footings and were then insulated with a mixture of Insulex and water. When the mixture was poured between the old wall and the new tile and wood walls an extra insulation was formed that helped keep room temperatures very mild in the summers and warm in the winters.

Next, an Annex was built 25 feet away from the main house with a second story bridge connecting the two buildings. Roman arches and ornate gates enclosed a tiled courtyard between the buildings.

Together, the Annex and the Main House contain three bedrooms; one was Scotty's, two suites; the Spanish Suite and the Johnson's suite; a solarium; a formal dining room; seven

bathrooms; two music rooms; an apartment for Mrs. Johnson; an office for Mr. Johnson; a spacious living hall; a gallery; a lanai and several other utility rooms.

The guest house; stable; cook house; gas station; chimes tower; powerhouse and the gate house, in approximately that order, were also constructed. A remodeling of the original garage was completed sometime during this phase of the construction.

During the height of the Castle's construction there were over one hundred workmen, skilled and

Above: Sundial detail showing the face of Janus. PHOTO JEFF FOOTT

Right: Chimes tower and tile clocks at Scotty's Castle on an October afternoon. The tile work at Death Valley Ranch was as finely crafted as any found in the mansions of California built during the same period.
PHOTO BY JEFF GNASS

otherwise, working on the Castle. Due to the remote location and severe weather conditions, hiring workers was a full time job. Wages for the workmen ranged from as much as $11 dollars a day for the skilled tile setters and carpenters to as low as $2.50 a day for the local Shoshone Indians hired for manual labor. Room and board was included for the Shoshone who lived in a segregated compound on the other side of Grapevine Canyon. Unskilled non-Indian laborer were paid $5.00 per day but were charged $1.50 a day for a room and $.50 for each meal.

The Johnson's were decent people who treated the Indians well and had steadfast rules for their workers. There was no drinking, gambling or mixing with the Indians by the white employees allowed.

When Mrs. Johnson was in residence at the Death Valley Ranch all white employees were expected to attend the Sunday worship services she performed. Any worker who did not attend Sunday services, or decided to break any of the Johnson's rules, was instantly terminated.

The remote location, harsh climate and the strict rules led to a fairly constant turnover in the Castle's labor force even though the wages were considered good for their day.

The enlarged main house was outfitted with only the finest furnishings available. Most of the furniture was custom made or imported from Europe. Every fixture and latch (there are no door knobs at the Castle) was designed and created specifically for Scotty's Castle.

Albert Johnson used the latest technology available in designing the Powerhouse used to supply the castle with electricity. He installed

a hydroelectric generating system and when spring water was piped at a rate of 200 gallons per minute into a 44,000 gallon reservoir it created enough water pressure to deliver a pressure rate of 95 pounds per square inch to a

Above: The gate between the Main House and Annex House is an intricate ironwork design which includes the detail of Johnson and Scott's initials (see page 39) in two of the panels. The JS logo can also be found on concrete fence posts surrounding the Castle.
PHOTO BY JEFF FOOTT

Pelton waterwheel that created a hydroelectric generating system that generated enough power to charge two separate banks of batteries. The Castle was run on the electricity provided by the energy stored in the two banks of batteries, a Fairbanks-Morse-110-volt DC generator and a Caterpillar standby generator. This system worked well until the Castle's need for energy increased and the DC diesel generators were replaced by a General Motors 440-volt AC generator during 1950s, which became the Castle's backup power source after commercial power was brought to the Castle in 1964.

A solar water heater was installed north of the main house in 1927. It heated water held in 960 feet of copper pipe under glass panels by sunlight and was piped into an insulated

storage tank to be distributed to the Castle. Although it was quite advanced for its era, it was never fully utilized to its full potential because of its poor performance. The system was quickly abandoned when propane became an available and inexpensive energy source.

The distinctive Chimes Tower, with its tiled clocks, was first designed by Johnson as a way to disguise hot water tanks. Instead, the 56 foot tower ended up holding a set of 25 different note chimes manufactured in Chicago. The largest of the chimes is a 12 foot long, 425 lb. "C" note and the smallest is a 120 lb. "C' that is just less than four feet long. The Chimes Tower could be heard to play a tune every fifteen minutes. The chimes' operations were controlled from the tower's second floor and were also wired to the roll player in the Lower Music Room and the organ in the Upper Music Room of the Main House.

A refreshing waterfall pouring over Jasper rock is located at one end of the Main Hall. The waterfall provided humidity to the dry air while the residents inside enjoyed the soothing sounds of gently falling water.

Perhaps the grandest showpiece in the whole Castle is the huge Welte-Mignon theater organ located in the Upper Music Room. The organ has over 1,121 pipes of all different sizes that include four sets of tune percussions, piano, flute, harp and other sounds including untuned percussions and even bird calls. It can also play the massive chimes in Chimes Tower. The organ was built to be played manually or mechanically by a Welte single-role player. In 1940, a Wurlitzer six-roll player was added. It is estimated that the original installation of the organ in the 1920s cost the Johnson's more than $50,000, a fortune at the time.

Unfortunately the crash of the stock market in 1929 and the Great Depression that followed eventually brought construction of the Castle

Below: The construction of Scotty's Castle began in 1922 and officially ended in 1931.
PHOTO COURTESY NATIONAL PARK SERVICE

to a halt. Construction officially ended in the spring of 1931, with the departure of the last workmen after Albert finally was forced by the Great Depression to stop building.

Johnson wasn't left completely destitute but he was no longer wealthy enough to spend millions of dollars on his Death Valley winter

Above: Detail of a balcony on the second-floor of the Main House at Scotty's Castle, Death Valley National Park, California.
PHOTO BY JEFF FOOTT

retreat. Construction of the 260 foot swimming pool was never completed, along with many of the more elaborate landscape plans. The Gate House attendant's apartment was also left in an incomplete state.

In 1932, Albert Johnson was shocked to discover that the land on which he'd built his Castle was not his own. When Johnson had originally purchased the land he did not check the accuracy of the description and location concerning the property lines. It was later discovered that due to a surveyor's error in the 1890s Johnson had unknowingly built his Castle northwest of his legal property line on property that was slated to become part of the Death Valley National Monument.

Nevada Congressman Samuel Arentz introduced a bill in 1933 to allow Johnson to buy the land. Both the House of Representatives and the Senate passed the bill but it was vetoed by President Franklin D. Roosevelt who felt the government should retain all mineral rights and have the right to purchase

Right: An arched doorway frames a view of the Main House at Scotty's Castle on an afternoon in October. Death Valley National Park.
PHOTO BY JEFF GNASS

the property if Johnson ever decided to sell. It took Castle Bill, H.R. 2476, passed in 1935, to allow Johnson to buy the property from the government, with a stipulation on the measure allowing the government first right of purchase should the Castle ever be sold.

During the 1930s, Scotty's Castle became a popular tourist attraction due to the growing popularity of the new national monument. Scotty could often be found sitting in his favorite chair near the entrance greeting guests and telling tales. Mysterious to the end, Scotty often retreated to his small shack at the Lower

Ranch, just a few miles away, whenever he needed privacy. The Lower Ranch, was built by Albert Johnson to secure the area's water rights and was without electricity and other modern appliances and conveniences.

After Albert Johnson's death in 1948, control of the Castle passed to the Gospel Foundation he had formed to control his assets after his death. Scotty moved to the Main House where he lived until he died in 1954.

In 1970, Scotty's Castle and Johnson's other Death Valley holdings were sold to the National Park Service by the Gospel Foundation.

DEATH VALLEY NATIONAL PARK

In 1994, President Clinton signed the Desert Protection Act into law, adding 1.3 million acres to Death Valley National Monument and changing its status to a national park. The newly acquired lands are the darker areas above.

Recent additions to Death Valley National Monument have increased its total area to more than 3.3 million acres, making it the largest National Park in the continental United States, and changing its designation from a national monument to a national park.

Death Valley National Monument came into existence on February 11, 1933, as President Herbert Hoover set aside 1,750,000 acres to preserve Death Valley for future generations. Four years later, on March 6, 1937, President Franklin D. Roosevelt added the 300,000 acres now known as the Nevada triangle to Death Valley National Monument.

Forty acres at Devil's Hole were added to Death Valley National Monument by President Harry S Truman on January 17, 1952, to protect a unique species of pupfish which evolved from a species stranded as Ice Age lakes retreated.

Scotty's Castle, its surrounding 1,500 acre Death Valley Ranch lands and the other Death Valley holdings once owned by Albert Johnson, were sold to the National Park Service by the Gospel Foundation of California in 1970 for $850,000, which included castle furnishings.

In 1976, Congress passed the Mining in the Parks Act which prohibited the filing of future mining claims in Death Valley and began to eliminate mining within the monument.

The United Nations recognized Death Valley National Monument as a part of the Mojave and Colorado Deserts Biosphere Reserve in 1984. International Biosphere Reserves, there are 43 in the United States, are areas dedicated to preserving ecological communities in their natural environment.

October 31, 1994, President William Clinton signed the Desert Protection Act into law which added 1.3 million acres to Death Valley National Monument and changed its official status to a national park. The 1994 Desert Protection Act protects 95% of Death Valley National Park as wilderness. The majority of the additional lands were added to the north and northwest areas of the national monument's boundaries.

Seventy-five thousand acres were added to the north of Scotty's Castle in the Death Valley Wash and the Last Chance Range. The mountains were named after a group of soldiers, led by Lt. David A Lyle, who were nearly out of water while searching for a route through the mountains in 1871. They stumbled upon the spring and named it "Last Chance Spring."

Eureka Valley, to the west of the Last Chance Range, added 200,000 acres to Death Valley National Park including the tallest sand dunes in California, some of which are nearly 700 feet high. The Eureka Valley addition protects three species of plants that are found nowhere else in the world: Eureka Dunegrass, Eureka Evening Primrose and Eureka Milk-vetch.

Saline Valley and Range lands added 400,000 acres to the park south of Eureka Valley and east of the Inyo Mountains. Salt mined in Saline Valley was so pure that no refining was necessary. Remnants of a tramway built in 1913 to haul salt over the mountains can still be seen along with a desert oasis.

Left: Lee Flat and the Nelson Range, a 50,000 acre parcel added to Death Valley National Park along the western boundary of the old national monument boundary.
PHOTO BY JEFF FOOTT

Right: Rainbow Canyon with bands of colored volcanic rocks in Death Valley National Park.
PHOTO BY TOM BEAN

DEATH VALLEY NATIONAL PARK CONTINUED...

50,000 additional acres were gained with the inclusion of Lee Flat and the Nelson Range along the western boundary of the old national monument boundary south of Saline Valley. Lee Flat is a plateau resting at 5,000 feet in elevation and includes a Joshua tree forest.

The Northern Panamint Valley to the west of Death Valley added another 100,000 acres to the national park including dunes, Rainbow Canyon, abandoned miners cabins and Darwin Falls. The desert oasis at Darwin Falls, which cascades into a year-round stream, provides a setting for one of the few riparian communities within Death Valley National Park.

The west side of the High Panamints, south of Highway 190 and east of Trona and Ballarat, added 100,000 acres including the ghost town of Panamint City. Ibex Hills and Saddle Peak Hills in the extreme southeastern part of the park added another 50,000 acres and several old mining ruins.

The Owlshead Mountains brought 125,000 acres from the southwestern boundary of Death Valley National Park to the north of the China Lake Naval Weapons Center. The area has two dry lake beds and old mining ruins.

The Greenwater Valley and Range south of Highway 190 and west of Highway 127, where 150,000 acres were added, was once home to Greenwater, a boom town that had a bank and two newspapers. Founded in 1905, the town grew to about 1000 residents by the early part of 1907, only to be nearly deserted by the end of the same year when the copper deposits proved to be shallow and the town went bust.

50,000 acres were added at Pyramid Peak, the highest peak in the Funeral Mountains, on the eastern boundary of the park. The area is accessible by foot from Highway 190 or by four-wheel drive on Hole-in-the-Wall Road.

The new additions to Death Valley National Park have added more than just 1.3 million acres to the boundaries of the the park, they have insured that these unique wilderness environments, unlike any others on earth, are preserved for generations to come.

Following Pages: Sand Dunes and rock-strewn desert floor in the Eureka Dunes 1994 addition to Death Valley National Park.
PHOTO BY JEFF FOOTT

Outside Back Cover: Dawn catches the Panamint Range and geometric salt evaporation patterns on the valley floor in Death Valley National Park.
PHOTO BY JACK DYKINGA

Below: Eureka Dunes, the tallest sand dunes in California, and the Last Chance Mountains.
PHOTO BY CARR CLIFTON

Right: Upper Darwin Falls cascades into a year-round stream in the Northern Panamint Valley.
PHOTO BY JEFF FOOTT